THE ILLUSTRATED
ENCYCLOPEDIA

VOLUME 4

G - I

Belitha Press

First published 1995 by
Macmillan Education Australia Pty Ltd

First published in the United Kingdom in 1995 by
Belitha Press Limited
31 Newington Green, London N16 9PU

Cataloguing in print data available from the British Library.

ISBN 1 85561 523 1 (Vol 4)
ISBN 1 85561 529 0 (Set)

Consultant: Frances Warhurst
UK editor: Maria O'Neill
Project editor: Jo Higgins

Typeset by Polar Design
Printed in Hong Kong

Acknowledgements

The author and publisher are grateful to the following for permission to reproduce copyright photographs:

Cover: The Photo Library

Australian Wool Corporation, p. 35 (left centre); Coo-ee Picture Library, pp. 5 (top right), 6 (right), 7 (bottom right), 13, 15, 19 (bottom), 23, 24 (top), 25, 27 (top left & bottom), 28, 31 (bottom), 33, 34, 35 (top), 36, 38, 40 (left), 41, 42 (top), 43 (bottom), 45 (top), 46 & 47 (bottom), 47, 49 (bottom), 52 (top), 53 (top), 54, 55, 59 (top left & right), 63 (bottom); CSIRO/Division of Entomology, p. 59 (left centre); Carole Ebhert, pp. 52 & 53 (bottom); John Higgins, pp. 6 (bottom), 14; NASA, p. 4; Natfoto/ A.N.T. Photo Library, p. 17; NHPA/A.N.T. Photo Library, p. 22; Northside Photographics, pp. 5 (bottom right), 21 (bottom left), 30 (right), 40 (centre), 43 (bottom), 44 (bottom left & right), 50 (bottom right) © Robert Moore,WBH, 51; Fred Mercay/ A.N.T. Photo Library, p. 49 (top); The Photo Library, pp. 21 (right), 53 (bottom right), 56 (top); Otto Rogge/A.N.T. Photo Library, pp. 20 (bottom right), 31 (bottom); Sporting Pix, pp. 45 (bottom), 57 (bottom); Silvestris/A.N.T. Photo Library, pp. 10 & 11 (centre), 18 (right), 39 (bottom); State Library of Victoria, p. 8; Wild Nature/A.N.T. Photo Library, p. 27 (bottom).

While every care has been taken to trace and acknowledge copyright the publishers tender their apologies for any accidental infringement where copyright has proved untraceable.

Illustrators
Sharyn Madder: 12, 13, 18, 19, 28, 29, 31, 39, 42, 43, 46, 47
Rhyll Plant: 4, 8, 9, 14, 15, 26, 27, 38, 56, 64
John Fairbridge: 10, 16, 34 (bottom), 41, 48, 49, 50, 51, 52, 53, 54, 60, 62
Paul Konye: 6, 7, 17, 30, 36, 40, 45, 57
Andrew Plant: 22, 23, 24, 25, 58, 59, 61
Xiangyi Mo: 32, 33, 34 (top), 37, 55

HOW TO USE THIS BOOK

The Illustrated Encyclopedia has over 300 entries. The entries are arranged alphabetically. To find your topic, use the guide letters at the top of each page to check you have the right volume. The first letter of your topic will be highlighted.

TOPIC: GOLD

guide letter

A B C D E F G H I J K L M

Use the guide words printed in the top right-hand corner of each page to find your topic. The guide words list the entries on a double-page spread. They are listed alphabetically. Check the guide words to see if you need to go backwards or forwards.

guide word

GOLD

You can also use the index in Volume 9 to find your topic.

gold
      Volume 4   10, **20–21**
      Volume 5   46–47

If you cannot find your topic in its alphabetical order in the encyclopedia, use the index.

gears
   see wheels

TOPIC: GEARS

The index lists all the topics in alphabetical order. It tells you where you will find your topic.

More information
on how to use the encyclopedia
and the index can be found
in Volume 9.

GALAXY

SEE ALSO
- Astronomy • Star
- Telescope • Universe

A galaxy is a huge collection of stars. Millions of galaxies make up the Universe. The Milky Way is our galaxy. The Earth and our Sun are part of the Milky Way.

THE MILKY WAY

There are so many stars in the Milky Way that they make a haze of light.

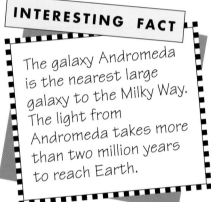

INTERESTING FACT

The galaxy Andromeda is the nearest large galaxy to the Milky Way. The light from Andromeda takes more than two million years to reach Earth.

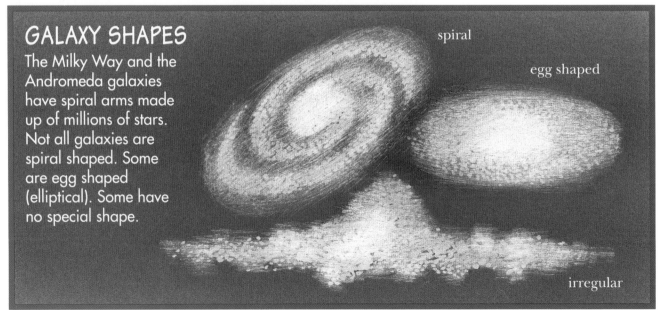

GALAXY SHAPES

The Milky Way and the Andromeda galaxies have spiral arms made up of millions of stars. Not all galaxies are spiral shaped. Some are egg shaped (elliptical). Some have no special shape.

spiral

egg shaped

irregular

GAMES

| SEE ALSO | • Computer • Doll • Hobby • Toy |

Games are fun to play. People have been playing games for hundreds of years. Some games can be played by one person; other games need two or more players.

OUTDOOR GAMES

Ball games and games such as hopscotch can help you learn throwing, catching and balancing skills.

Running and chasing games use lots of energy. You can learn to play together and get lots of exercise when you play these games.

CARD GAMES

A good memory is handy when you play card games. There are 52 cards in a pack.

INDOOR GAMES

Many board games involve luck and taking chances. Players take turns to throw the dice and move around the board.

Indoor games are great fun when the weather is too cold, too hot or too wet. You can use your imagination to play word games. You need to think ahead to make different moves when you play games such as draughts and chess.

HISTORY

Chess is one of the oldest board games. It came from a game played in India more than 1400 years ago.

GARDEN

SEE ALSO • Compost • Flower • Plant • Vegetable

A garden is a place where plants grow. Flowers, fruit and vegetables are grown in gardens. Some gardens are small while others are large.

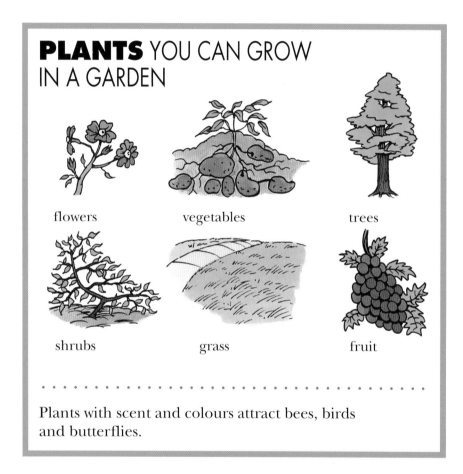

PLANTS YOU CAN GROW IN A GARDEN

flowers

vegetables

trees

shrubs

grass

fruit

Plants with scent and colours attract bees, birds and butterflies.

◀ **FAMOUS GARDENS**
There are many famous gardens in towns and cities all over the world.

GARDEN

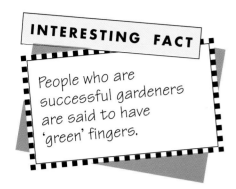

HISTORY

Long ago, grand houses and palaces had many large gardens. These gardens often had fountains, pools, terraces and statues.

◀ BOTANIC GARDENS

Gardens that grow many different kinds of plants are called botanic gardens.

GARDENERS ▼

Gardeners decide what to plant in a garden. They make sure that plants get enough light, soil, water and food to survive.

A gardener digs the soil. Then, a gardener sows seeds and plants seedlings. The gardener looks after the plants while they are growing.

TOOLS

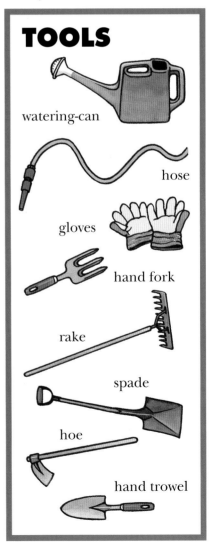

watering-can

hose

gloves

hand fork

rake

spade

hoe

hand trowel

GAS

SEE ALSO • Air • Fossil • Fuel • Oil

Gas is all around us, but we cannot see it. There are many different gases. The most important gases for life are oxygen and carbon dioxide. Some gases are used as fuel. Natural gas is used for cooking, lighting and heating.

GASES IN THE AIR

Air is a mixture of gases.

• We breathe in oxygen from the air. We breathe out carbon dioxide.

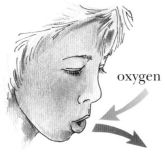

oxygen

carbon dioxide

• Plants take in carbon dioxide. They put oxygen back into the air.

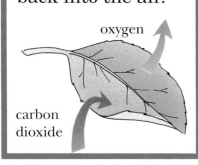

oxygen

carbon dioxide

HISTORY

Long ago, lights were run on gas made from coal.

LIQUID GAS

Gas turns into liquid when it is cold enough or under high pressure. Some cars and trucks use liquid gas for fuel.

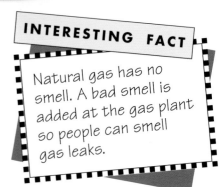

INTERESTING FACT

Natural gas has no smell. A bad smell is added at the gas plant so people can smell gas leaks.

HOW GAS IS FORMED

Natural gas is formed under the Earth's surface. It was formed over millions of years from the remains of dead plants and animals.

1. Dead sea plants and animals form a layer on the seabed.

2. They are covered with a layer of mud. The mud turns to rock.

3. The heat and pressure from the rock change the dead remains into oil and then gas.

WHERE GAS IS FOUND

Gas deposits found beneath the Earth's surface are mined by drilling rigs. Gas deposits found beneath the sea are mined offshore by drilling rigs.

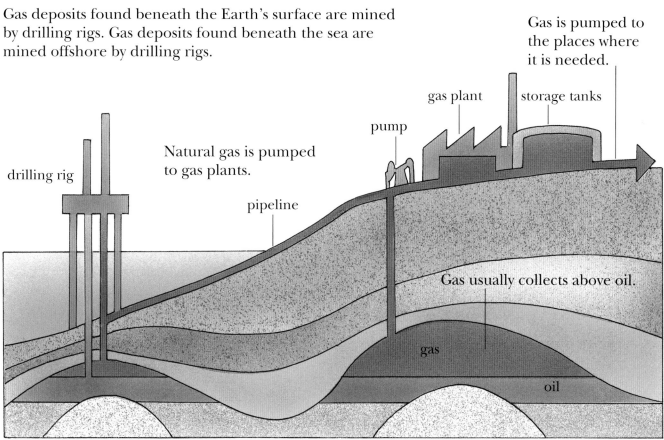

Gas is pumped to the places where it is needed.

gas plant   storage tanks

pump

Natural gas is pumped to gas plants.

drilling rig

pipeline

Gas usually collects above oil.

gas

oil

GEM

SEE ALSO • Minerals • Mining • Quartz

A gem is a precious stone. Gems are used to make jewellery. They are cut and polished and set in metals such as gold and silver. They are also used to decorate objects.

KINDS OF GEMS

diamond   ruby   emerald

sapphire   turquoise   lapis lazuli

HISTORY

Gems have been used to make crown jewels for kings and queens.

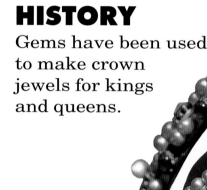

The finest jewels are diamonds. Diamonds are transparent stones. They are beautiful to look at because of the way they reflect light.

WHERE GEMS ARE FOUND ▶
Most gems are found in different kinds of rocks.

INTERESTING FACT
Diamonds are the hardest substance. They are used to cut and grind other hard substances.

JEWELLERY
Gemstones are cut into different shapes to make jewellery.

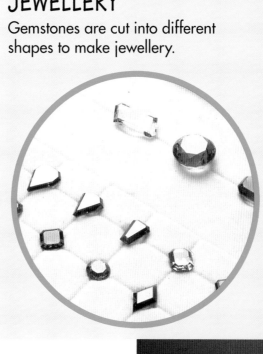

GIRAFFE

SEE ALSO • Animal • Grassland • Mammal • Ungulates

A giraffe is a mammal. It is the tallest animal on Earth. It has long legs and a long neck.

PARTS OF A GIRAFFE

Average height (male): 5.5 metres
Average weight (male): 900 kilograms

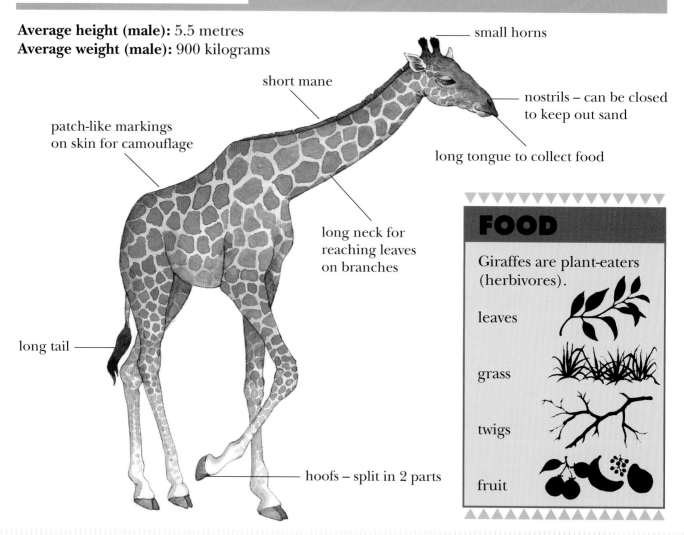

small horns

short mane

nostrils – can be closed to keep out sand

patch-like markings on skin for camouflage

long tongue to collect food

long neck for reaching leaves on branches

long tail

hoofs – split in 2 parts

FOOD

Giraffes are plant-eaters (herbivores).

leaves

grass

twigs

fruit

WHERE GIRAFFES LIVE

● Most giraffes live on the African grasslands.

HOW A GIRAFFE MOVES

• A giraffe has to spread its front legs and lower its head to eat and drink from the ground.
• To walk, a giraffe moves both legs on one side of its body and then both legs on the other side.
• To gallop, both back legs swing out together and land in front of the front legs. A giraffe can gallop at a very fast speed.

HOW
GIRAFFES LIVE

• A giraffe usually gives birth to one calf at a time.
• A calf is about two metres tall when it is born. It can stand up within one hour.
• The female giraffe (a cow) feeds her young with milk for nine to ten months.
• Giraffes live in small herds.
• A giraffe can live for 15 to 20 years.

INTERESTING FACT

A giraffe only has seven neck bones, like other mammals.

GLACIER

SEE ALSO • Iceberg • River

A glacier is a river of ice. It moves very slowly.
Glaciers are formed high up in the mountains.

INTERESTING FACT

Boulders and stones in a glacier can form a dam when the glacier melts.

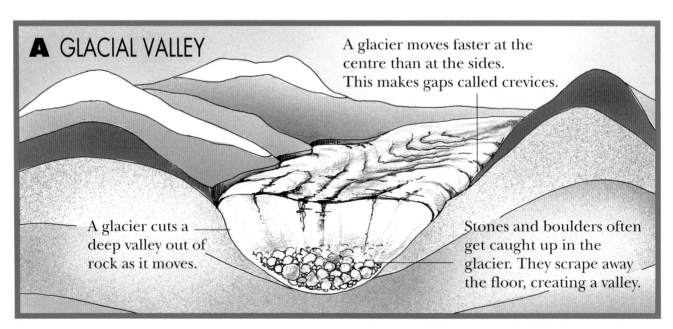

A GLACIAL VALLEY

A glacier moves faster at the centre than at the sides. This makes gaps called crevices.

A glacier cuts a deep valley out of rock as it moves.

Stones and boulders often get caught up in the glacier. They scrape away the floor, creating a valley.

MOUNTAIN SPORTS

Mountaineers climb glaciers.

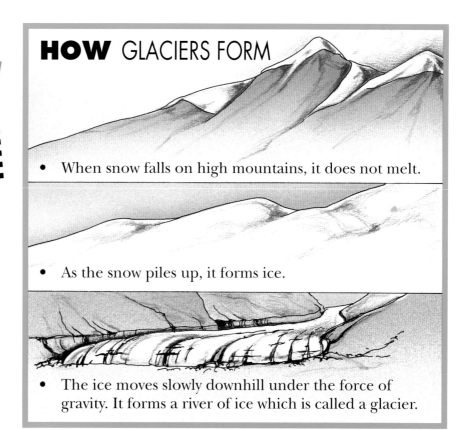

HOW GLACIERS FORM

- When snow falls on high mountains, it does not melt.

- As the snow piles up, it forms ice.

- The ice moves slowly downhill under the force of gravity. It forms a river of ice which is called a glacier.

GLASS

SEE ALSO • Recycling

Glass is a hard material that you can see through. It is made by heating sand, soda and lime. When glass is melted, it can be made into any shape.

HOW BOTTLES ARE MADE

Glass bottles are made by placing hot glass in a mould. Air is blown into the mould to push the glass out into the shape.

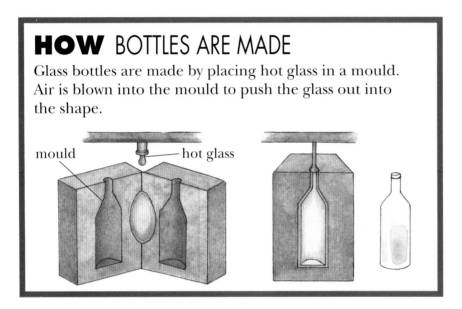

mould   hot glass

USES OF GLASS

Glass is used to make many different things. Special ingredients can be added to glass to make it tougher, heat-proofed or coloured.

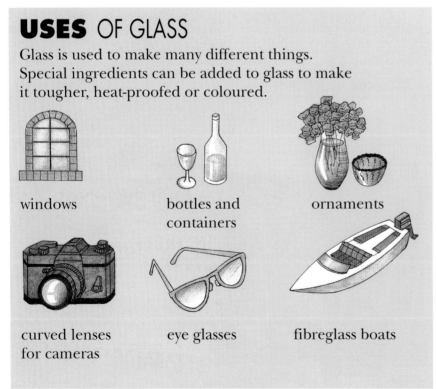

windows

bottles and containers

ornaments

curved lenses for cameras

eye glasses

fibreglass boats

GLASS BLOWING ▼

A glass blower makes beautiful objects by blowing down a tube into a lump of soft, hot glass. The lump of glass is heated in a furnace.

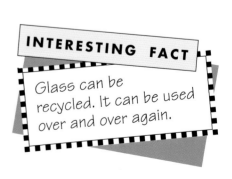

INTERESTING FACT

Glass can be recycled. It can be used over and over again.

GLIDER

SEE ALSO • Aeroplane • Hang-gliding

A glider is an aircraft. It uses air currents to glide and soar in the air. It does not have an engine for power.

LAUNCHING A GLIDER

A glider has no power of its own. It must be pulled by something until it is going fast enough to fly alone. It can be launched by a power winch, car or aeroplane.

INTERESTING FACT

Gliders can be used in sport, flight training and research.

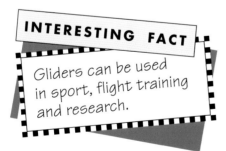

HOW A GLIDER FLIES

A glider can fly silently anywhere as long as it can catch rising currents of warm air.

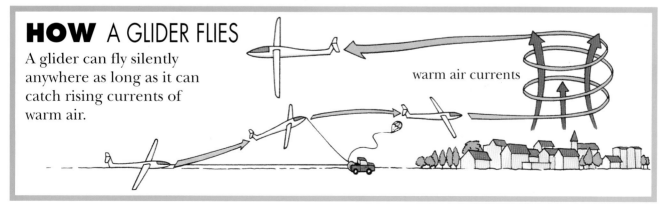

warm air currents

GOAT

SEE ALSO • Animal • Farming • Mammal • Ungulates

A goat is a mammal. It belongs to the same family as sheep and cows. There are wild goats and goats which are kept as farm animals.

PARTS OF A GOAT

hollow horns

hair

short tail

beard

long, thin straight legs

cloven hoofs divided into 2

Average height: 1 metre
Average weight: 45 to 90 kilograms

WILD GOATS

Wild goats such as ibexes and markhors live mainly in rocky and mountainous places. They eat plants and need little water.

WHERE WILD GOATS LIVE

● Asia
■ Europe
◆ North America

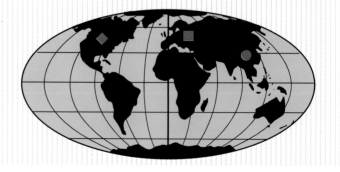

FOOD

Goats are plant-eaters (herbivores).

twigs

grass

shrubs

leaves

FARM GOATS

Farm goats live in all parts of the world. Farmers raise goats to produce milk, meat, wool and skins. Cashmere and Angora goats produce valuable hair which is woven into cloth.

HOW GOATS LIVE

• A female goat gives birth to one to three kids at the same time.
• Kids are born with hair and with their eyes open. They can run and jump within six hours.
• The female goat feeds the kids with milk from her teats for three to six months.
• After six months, the kids can find their own food.
• Goats live for 10 to 14 years.

GOLD

SEE ALSO • Metal • Mining

Gold is a soft, yellow metal. It does not rust. Gold has always been valuable because it is a scarce metal.

HISTORY ▶

In the past, the discovery of gold led to gold rushes. Thousands of people rushed to where gold had been found, hoping to become rich.

GOLD MINES

Gold is found in rock. Miners go underground to mine for gold. Some gold is found on the surface of the ground.

GOLD NUGGETS

Gold nuggets and smaller grains of gold are sometimes found in streams near goldfields.

WHERE GOLD IS FOUND

- ● South Africa
- ■ Russia
- ◆ Australia
- ★ Canada
- ▲ United States

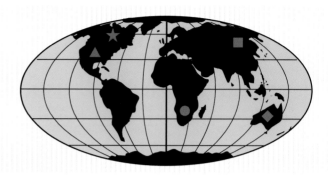

GOLD INGOTS

Melted gold is poured into moulds to make bricks of gold called ingots. Gold ingots are very valuable and are kept in banks.

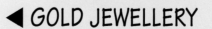

◀ GOLD JEWELLERY

Gold has always been used to make jewellery and objects for people.

GOLDFISH

SEE ALSO • Animal • Fish • Pet

A goldfish is a small fish. It belongs to the carp family. Some goldfish can be gold in colour. Others can be a mixture of gold, black and white. Goldfish are easy pets to keep.

PARTS OF A GOLDFISH

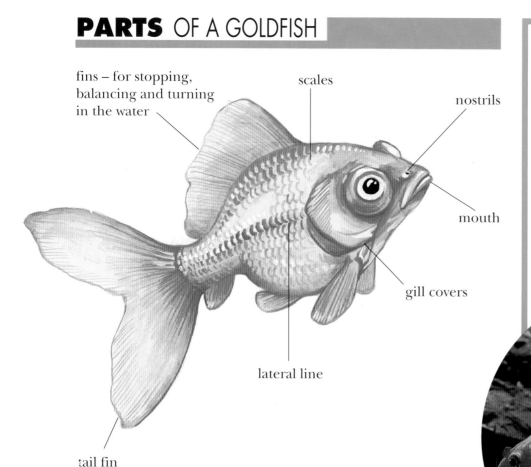

fins – for stopping, balancing and turning in the water

scales

nostrils

mouth

gill covers

lateral line

tail fin

Average length:
5 to 10 centimetres. Some goldfish grow up to 30 centimetres long.

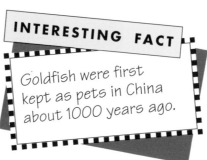

INTERESTING FACT

Goldfish were first kept as pets in China about 1000 years ago.

A PET GOLDFISH

A goldfish needs:
- an aquarium or pond with a large surface area. Oxygen from the air can dissolve in the water.
- regular food.
- fresh water and a clean aquarium or pond.
- plenty of space for swimming.

Rocks and plants make an interesting home for goldfish.

HOW GOLDFISH LIVE

• The female goldfish lays eggs which are fertilized by the male.
• A female will lay up to 2000 eggs. The eggs stick to plants in the water.
• The eggs hatch in three to ten days.
• The young fry eat their yolk sac for the first few days. Then they swim by themselves and gradually eat dried food.
• Goldfish may live for 20 years.

KINDS OF GOLDFISH

There are many different kinds of goldfish.

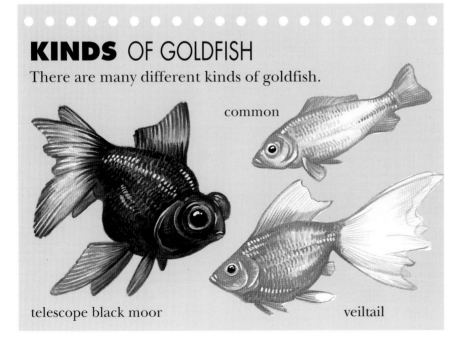

common

telescope black moor

veiltail

FOOD

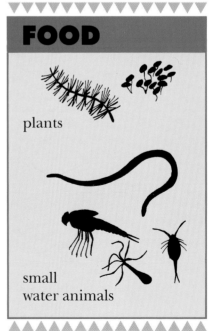

plants

small water animals

23

GRASS

SEE ALSO • Grassland • Plant

Grass is a plant. It grows very quickly. There are over 10 000 different kinds of grass. Grass grows in most parts of the world.

PARTS OF GRASS

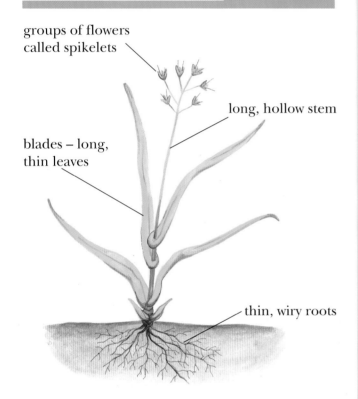

groups of flowers called spikelets

long, hollow stem

blades – long, thin leaves

thin, wiry roots

CEREAL GRASSES

Wheat, rice, millet, corn, barley and oats are cereal grasses. They are an important source of food. Cereal grasses are grown by people all over the world.

◄ When grass is destroyed by fire, eaten by animals or mowed by machines, it will still grow if the roots are left.

24

HOW GRASS GROWS

flower head

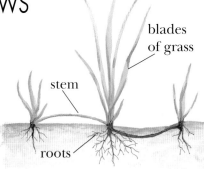
blades of grass

stem

roots

- Most grasses are pollinated by the wind. They grow from seeds dropped by the flower head.

- Some grasses grow from underground roots. Other grasses grow from stems which run along the ground.

BAMBOO ▼

Bamboo is a woody kind of grass. Bamboo can grow up to 30 metres high. It can be used for building houses, bridges, rafts and furniture.

HAY ▶

Some animals eat grass. They eat fresh grass in summer and dried grass in winter. Dried grass is called hay.

GRASS HABITAT

Grass provides insects such as grasshoppers with a place to live. Insects provide food for larger animals such as anteaters.

GRASSHOPPER

SEE ALSO • Animal • Insect • Life Cycle

A grasshopper is an insect that can jump and fly. Grasshoppers live in most parts of the world. They live in places where there are plenty of green plants to eat.

PARTS OF A GRASSHOPPER

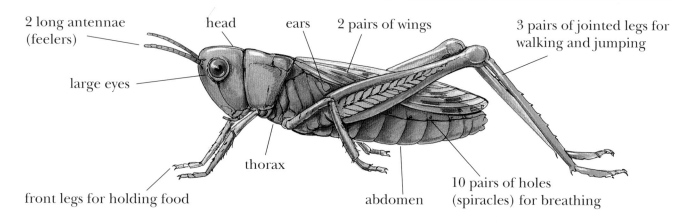

2 long antennae (feelers)

head

ears

2 pairs of wings

3 pairs of jointed legs for walking and jumping

large eyes

thorax

front legs for holding food

abdomen

10 pairs of holes (spiracles) for breathing

LIFE CYCLE OF A GRASSHOPPER

- Female grasshoppers dig a hole in soil or plant material and lay their eggs.
- Larvae or nymphs hatch from the eggs. They look like adult grasshoppers without wings.
- Each nymph sheds its skin (moults) and grows a new skin five or six times before becoming a winged adult.

FOOD

- Some grasshoppers will only eat certain kinds of green plants.
- Other grasshoppers will eat any kind of green plant they can find.

INTERESTING FACT

The male long-horned grasshopper sings to attract a mate and warn off rivals. It rubs the base of its front wings together.

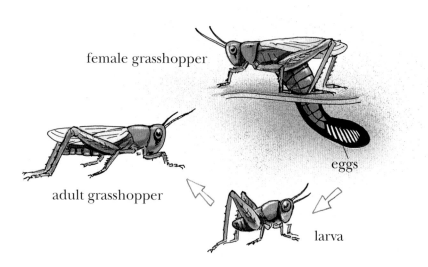

female grasshopper

eggs

adult grasshopper

larva

26

KINDS OF GRASSHOPPERS

There are two kinds of grasshoppers.

Short-horned grass-hoppers have short feelers. Locusts are short-horned grasshoppers.

- They may be brown, black, grey, red or yellow.
- Some have brightly coloured wings.
- Their ears are on the body under the wings.

Long-horned grasshoppers have long feelers.

- They are usually green. Some are brown, black or grey.
- Most live on the ground, but some live in trees.
- Their ears are below the knee joints on their front legs.

HOW A GRASSHOPPER MOVES

Many grasshoppers can jump long distances. When a grasshopper jumps, its wings are open. When it lands, it closes its wings.

INTERESTING FACT

The male short-horned grasshopper also sings to attract a mate and warn off rivals. It rubs its back legs against its front wings.

LOCUST ▼ SWARMS

Locusts can breed very quickly. They can form into large swarms and move from one place to another. Locust swarms can cause great damage to crops and green plants.

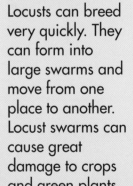

GRASSLAND

SEE ALSO
• Ecology • Grass
• Ungulates • Vulture

A grassland is an area of land where grass is the main plant. Grasslands provide homes and food for many different kinds of plant-eating animals. Natural grasslands are found on all continents of the world except Antarctica.

FEEDING ON THE AFRICAN SAVANNA

A savanna is a grassland. Many different kinds of wild animals feed on the African savanna. Some animals share the same kind of plant.

- Gazelles nibble tender leaves close to the ground.
- Zebras eat the tougher stems on the upper parts of the grasses.

giraffes

elephants

Thompson gazelles

FARMLANDS

Many grasslands are used for farmland. They are used to grow crops for food. Grasslands planted with richer grasses provide food for cattle and sheep.

A GRASSLAND ECOSYSTEM

A grassland ecosystem is made up of living and non-living things that all work together and depend on each other.

- A plant community.
- An animal community.
- Non-living things such as the Sun, rain, air and minerals.
- Fungi and bacteria that live in the soil.

There are not many trees on grasslands. Many animals and some birds dig burrows in the ground for shelter and safety.

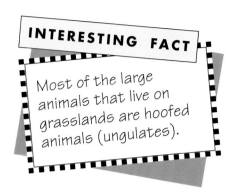

INTERESTING FACT

Most of the large animals that live on grasslands are hoofed animals (ungulates).

white-backed vulture

zebras

hyenas

white rhinoceroses

cape buffaloes

lions

NOMADIC ▶ SHEPHERDS

Nomadic shepherds live on some grasslands. Nomadic people move around to find food for their animals.

29

GRAVITY

| SEE ALSO | • Astronaut • Moon • Tides • Universe |

Gravity is a pulling force. The Earth's gravity keeps us from flying off into space.

When we throw a ball up into the air, gravity pulls it down.

When we jump in the air, gravity pulls us down.

CENTRE OF GRAVITY

The centre of gravity is the point of an object or person where there is as much weight on one side as on the other.

When you find the centre of gravity in an object, you can get that object to balance.

If two balls with different weights are dropped at the same time and from the same height, they will both reach the ground at the same time.

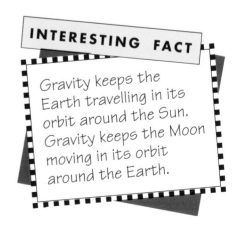

INTERESTING FACT

Gravity keeps the Earth travelling in its orbit around the Sun. Gravity keeps the Moon moving in its orbit around the Earth.

GUINEA PIG

SEE ALSO
• Animal • Mammal • Pet
• Rodents

A guinea pig is a mammal. It belongs to a group of animals called rodents. Guinea pigs are popular pets.

PARTS OF A GUINEA PIG

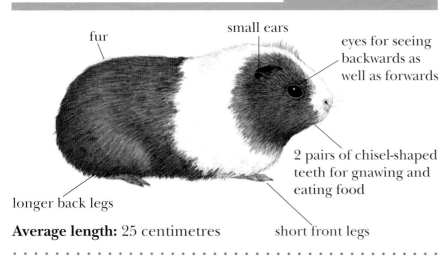

fur

small ears

eyes for seeing backwards as well as forwards

2 pairs of chisel-shaped teeth for gnawing and eating food

longer back legs

short front legs

Average length: 25 centimetres

HOW GUINEA PIGS LIVE

• A female guinea pig usually gives birth to one to four young at a time.
• The mother guinea pig feeds her young with milk for two to four weeks.
• Guinea pigs communicate using high-pitched squeaks. They make chattering noises by grinding their teeth.

A PET GUINEA PIG

• Guinea pigs need a warm, dry hutch with plenty of room to move around.
• Place the hutch where the air temperature is even all year round.
• They need fresh food and water every day.
• Clean the hutch once a day.

INTERESTING FACT

A guinea pig is also called a cavy.

FOOD

Guinea pigs are herbivores. They only eat plant food such as grass, hay, corn and other green plants.

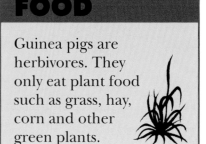

GYMNASTICS

SEE ALSO • Exercise • Olympic Games

Gymnastics is a series of exercises. They help to keep you fit and healthy. Gymnastics is made up of exercises you can do on the floor and exercises you can do using equipment.

BALANCING AND TUMBLING SKILLS
Balancing and tumbling skills are used over and over again in gymnastics.

forward roll

backward roll

cartwheel

walkover

scale

Y scale

WARM-UP SESSIONS

Gymnasts stretch and loosen their muscles before practising gymnastics.

A routine is a combination of tumbling, balance and dance movements. The movements are performed one after another without stopping. It is important to practise routines on the floor before you do them on equipment.

KINDS OF GYMNASTICS

There are many kinds of gymnastics.

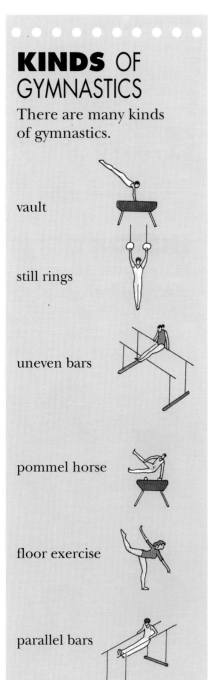

vault

still rings

uneven bars

pommel horse

floor exercise

parallel bars

THE OLYMPIC GAMES ▶

Many gymnasts compete in the Olympic Games.

STILL RINGS ▼

Only men compete in the still rings event at the Olympic Games. Judges want to see as little movement as possible in the rings when the gymnasts are performing.

BALANCE BEAM ▶

Gymnasts can lie, stand or lean over any part of the balance beam. They must not touch the support legs of the balance beam or the floor.

HAIR

SEE ALSO
• Animal • Camouflage
• Mammal • Skin

Hair grows from the skin of all mammals. It provides warmth and protection. Hair can be thick or thin, short or long, straight, wavy or curly.

PARTS OF A HAIR FOLLICLE

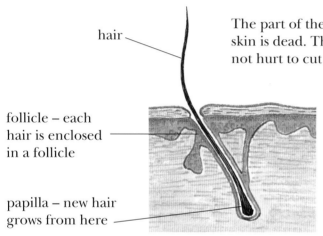

hair

The part of the hair outside the skin is dead. This is why it does not hurt to cut hair.

follicle – each hair is enclosed in a follicle

The part of the hair under the skin is living.

papilla – new hair grows from here

INTERESTING FACT

A human's scalp hair usually grows 1 to 2.5 centimetres every two months.

PROTECTIVE HAIR

Thick, flat hair on a seal protects it against cuts from sharp rocks.

HISTORY

Hairstyles are always changing. They go in and out of fashion like clothes do.

TACTILE HAIR

Some animals such as cats have sensitive hairs called whiskers. Whiskers help animals feel their way through narrow or dark places.

Fur is soft, thick hair that covers the bodies of some animals such as rabbits, tigers and bears. The colour and patterns of some fur provide camouflage. ▶

USEFUL HAIR

Sheep's hair is called fleece. It is woven to make woollen material.

QUILLS

Porcupines, hedgehogs and echidnas have sharp, spiny hairs called quills. Quills are used for protection.

HANG-GLIDING

SEE ALSO
• Aeroplane • Air • Balloon
• Glider

Hang-gliding is a popular sport. Hang-gliders fly by gliding on air currents. The pilot is held by a harness and trapeze bar to the hang-glider.

PARTS OF A HANG-GLIDER

A hang-glider pilot should wear protective clothing.

wings

tail

harness

trapeze bar

helmet

INTERESTING FACT

A hang-glider has light wings – 22 to 44 kilograms in weight. This makes the hang-glider light to carry.

◄ TAKE-OFF

Hang-glider pilots jump from a high place such as a hill, cliff or mountain. They use their body weight to control the hang-glider in the air.

HEART

SEE ALSO • Animal • Blood • Exercise
              • Human Body

The heart is a strong muscle. It pumps blood which carries food and oxygen around the body. All animals have a heart.

PARTS OF THE HEART

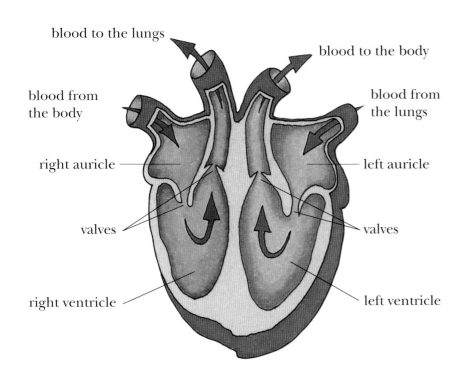

blood to the lungs

blood to the body

blood from the body

blood from the lungs

right auricle

left auricle

valves

valves

right ventricle

left ventricle

EXERCISE ▲
Exercise makes the heart beat faster. This helps to keep our bodies healthy.

HOW A HEART WORKS

The heart has four parts – two parts on each side. Each side works independently.
• On the left side, fresh blood carrying oxygen from the lungs enters the left auricle. The blood is forced through a valve (a kind of gate) down to the left ventricle. The valve closes after the blood has gone through. This stops the blood flowing backwards. The oxygen-rich blood is then pumped from the heart to the head and body.
• On the right side, stale blood carrying wastes such as carbon dioxide enters the right auricle and passes into the right ventricle. It is pumped out to the lungs where it will leave carbon dioxide and pick up oxygen.

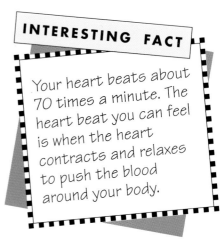

INTERESTING FACT

Your heart beats about 70 times a minute. The heart beat you can feel is when the heart contracts and relaxes to push the blood around your body.

HEAT

SEE ALSO • Clothing • Coal • Fuel • Oil • Sun

Heat is a form of energy. You can feel heat, but you cannot see it. All life on Earth needs heat from the Sun. To make heat, people burn fuels such as coal or oil.

BODY HEAT

• Your body uses food to produce heat to keep you warm.
• In cold weather, you need to wear warm clothes to keep in your body heat.
• In hot weather, you need to wear cool clothes to let unwanted body heat escape.

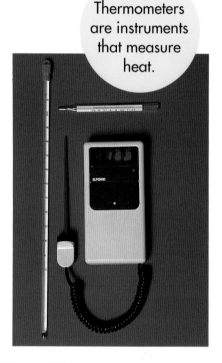

Thermometers are instruments that measure heat.

 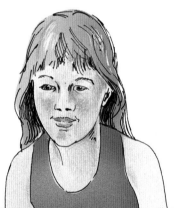

HEAT TRAVELS IN THREE WAYS

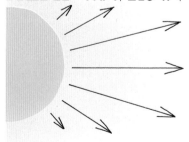

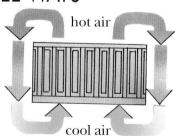
hot air
cool air

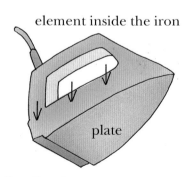
element inside the iron
plate

Radiation
Hot objects give off heat. Heat from the Sun travels through space by radiation.

Convection
Heat is moved from one place to another by moving air. Hot air from a heater rises. Cool air is sucked in to replace the warm air.

Conduction
Heat travels through objects. In an iron, heat travels from the hottest part (the element) to the coolest part (the plate).

HEDGEHOG

SEE ALSO • Animal • Mammal • Hair

A hedgehog is a small animal covered in spines.
The sharp spines protect it from its enemies.
When in danger, a hedgehog tucks in its head
and feet, and rolls itself into a ball.

PARTS OF A HEDGEHOG

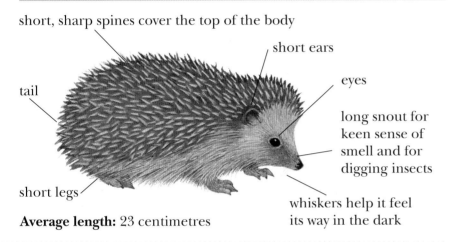

short, sharp spines cover the top of the body

short ears

eyes

long snout for
keen sense of
smell and for
digging insects

tail

short legs

whiskers help it feel
its way in the dark

Average length: 23 centimetres

FOOD

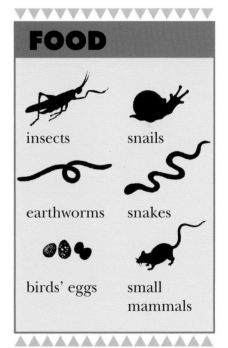

insects

snails

earthworms

snakes

birds' eggs

small
mammals

WHERE HEDGEHOGS LIVE

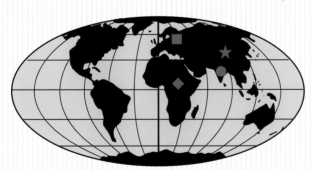

- ● **India**
- ■ **Europe**
- ◆ **Africa**
- ★ **West Asia**

HOW HEDGEHOGS LIVE

- Hedgehogs rest in burrows during the day.
At night they come out to hunt for food.
- A female hedgehog gives birth to two to ten
young once or twice a year.
- Hedgehogs hibernate in winter. They roll into
a ball, and sleep in shelters lined with grass
and leaves.

HELICOPTER

A helicopter is a type of aircraft. It can fly upwards, downwards, forwards and sideways.

SEE ALSO • Aeroplane • Transport

PARTS OF A HELICOPTER

Rotor blades act as propeller and wings. They are curved on top and flat on the bottom like the wings of an aeroplane.

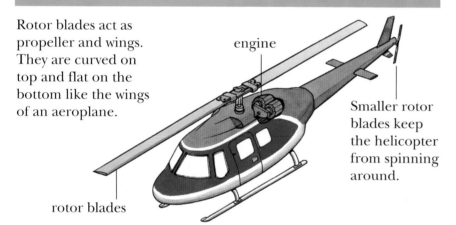

engine

Smaller rotor blades keep the helicopter from spinning around.

rotor blades

HANDY IN SMALL SPACES

Helicopters can be used to rescue people who are stranded.

Helicopters can move straight up and down. They are used to land in difficult places.

HOW A HELICOPTER FLIES

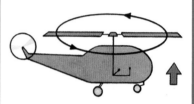

Going up
Level rotor blades make the helicopter fly upwards. The engine turns the rotor blades very quickly. They give power for take-off.

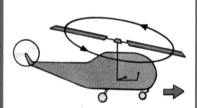

Going forwards
The pilot tilts the rotor blades forwards. The engine turns the rotor blades very quickly so the helicopter can fly forwards.

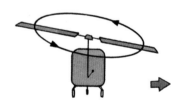

Going sideways
The pilot tilts the rotor blades to one side. This moves the helicopter to that side.

HERITAGE

SEE ALSO
• Conservation • Ecology
• National Park

Heritage is special things and places that people value and care about. It is the things and places that people agree are worth keeping and looking after for future generations.

Our heritage can tell us how people lived their lives in the past.

FOLKLORE

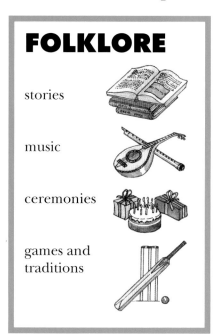

stories

music

ceremonies

games and traditions

MOVEABLE OBJECTS

inkwell   teddy bear   old lamp   old boots   tram (or car or train)

THINGS MADE BY PEOPLE

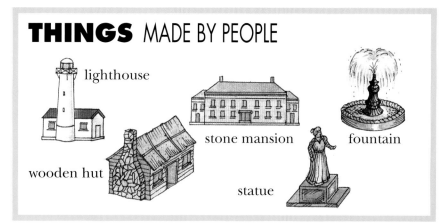

lighthouse

stone mansion   fountain

wooden hut

statue

NATURAL PLACES

Natural places are also part of our heritage. They include the habitats of plants and animals, fossil sites, rock art and ceremonial sites, wetlands and forests.

◄ Yosemite National Park in USA is on the World Heritage List. The World Heritage List is a list of places that a group of countries have agreed to save and look after for all time.

HIPPOPOTAMUS

SEE ALSO
• Animal • Mammal
• Ungulates

A hippopotamus is a large animal that lives on land and in water. It spends most of its time in water and can swim and dive. On land, a hippopotamus can run quickly.

PARTS OF A COMMON HIPPOPOTAMUS

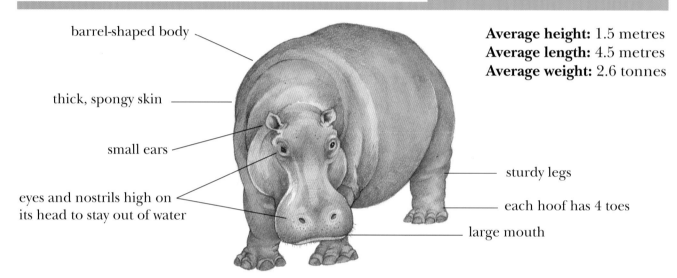

barrel-shaped body

thick, spongy skin

small ears

eyes and nostrils high on its head to stay out of water

Average height: 1.5 metres
Average length: 4.5 metres
Average weight: 2.6 tonnes

sturdy legs

each hoof has 4 toes

large mouth

WHERE HIPPOPOTAMUSES LIVE

Hippopotamuses live near rivers, lakes and swamps.
● **Africa**

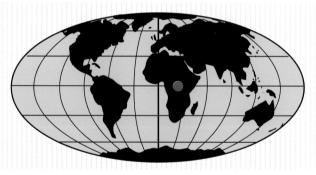

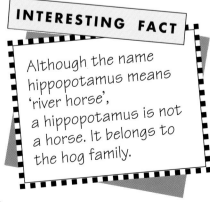

INTERESTING FACT

Although the name hippopotamus means 'river horse', a hippopotamus is not a horse. It belongs to the hog family.

FOOD

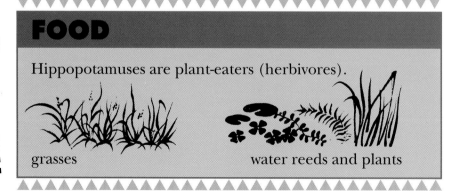

Hippopotamuses are plant-eaters (herbivores).

grasses

water reeds and plants

KINDS OF HIPPOPOTAMUSES

There are two kinds of hippopotamuses – the common hippopotamus and the pygmy hippopotamus.

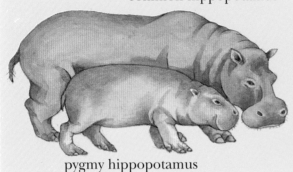

common hippopotamus

pygmy hippopotamus

THE PYGMY HIPPOPOTAMUS

- The pygmy hippopotamus is much smaller than the common hippopotamus. It is about 75 centimetres tall and 1.8 metres long. It weighs 180 to 270 kilograms.
- The pygmy hippopotamus can stay out of water for a very long time.
- The pygmy hippopotamus is much rarer than the common hippopotamus.

HOW A HIPPOPOTAMUS LIVES

- Hippopotamuses live in family groups or herds.
- They spend their day in water floating or walking along the river bottom. At night, they come ashore to feed.

- The mother usually has one baby at a time and takes it into the water as soon as it is born.
- The mother often carries the baby on her back in the water.
- A hippopotamus is fully grown at six years. It can live for up to 30 years.

HOBBY

SEE ALSO • Dancing • Games • Horse Riding • Watersports

A hobby is an activity you can enjoy in your leisure time. The hobby you choose depends on where you live and the sorts of things you like to do.

COLLECTING

People can collect things as a hobby. Stamp-collecting is a very popular hobby.

OUTDOOR ▼ HOBBIES

Some hobbies such as birdwatching and fishing are outdoor activities. Some such as swimming or basketball are physical activities.

CREATIVE HOBBIES

Many people enjoy hobbies where they can draw, write, paint or take photographs.

Many people ▲ make things as a hobby.

HOBBY CLUBS ▼

People often form clubs and groups so they can get together to talk about and share their hobbies.

HOCKEY

Hockey is a sport. It is played with two teams on a field. Players use a curved stick to hit a small ball into the other team's goal. Ice hockey is played on ice.

SEE ALSO
• Olympic Games
• Ice Skating

HOW TO PLAY HOCKEY

- Players hit, trap and dribble the ball with the hockey stick. The ball can only be moved with a stick.
- A goal keeper is allowed to kick the ball or stop it with any part of the body while the ball is in play.

ICE HOCKEY ▼

Ice hockey is played on ice. Players skate up and down the rink and shoot the puck with their sticks into the other team's goal. Players wear special padded clothing to protect themselves.

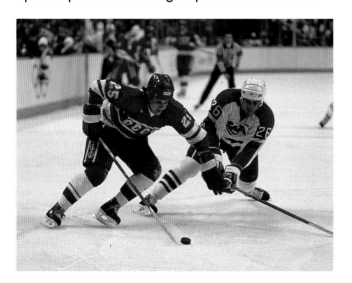

DIFFERENCES BETWEEN HOCKEY AND ICE HOCKEY

- Hockey has two teams of 11 players. Ice hockey has two teams of six players.
- Hockey has two halves of 35 minutes. Ice hockey has three periods of 20 minutes.
- Hockey players use a curved stick. Ice hockey players use a long-handled stick which has a curved blade.
- A hockey ball is about 23.5 centimetres in circumference. Ice hockey is played with a flat rubber disc called a puck.

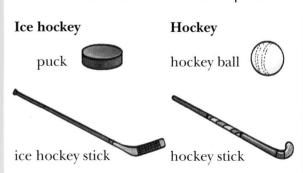

Ice hockey	Hockey
puck	hockey ball
ice hockey stick	hockey stick

HORSE

SEE ALSO
• Animal • Horse Riding
• Mammal • Pet • Ungulates

A horse is a strong animal that can run very fast. Horses were one of the first wild animals to be tamed by people. People could use horses for riding, and heavy work such as ploughing and pulling carts.

PARTS OF A HORSE

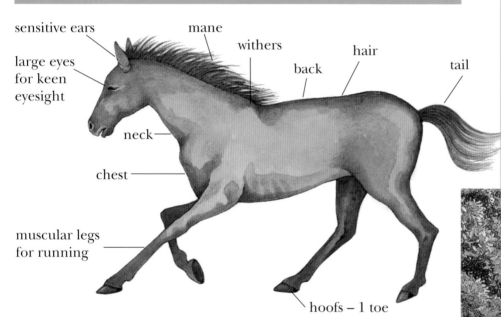

sensitive ears

mane

withers

back

hair

tail

large eyes for keen eyesight

neck

chest

muscular legs for running

hoofs – 1 toe

Average weight: 450 kilograms
Average height (from withers): 170 centimetres

FOOD

Horses are plant-eaters (herbivores).

grass

oats

rolled barley

bran

beets

hay

HISTORY ▼

Long ago, horses pulled different kinds of transport. Today, cars, trucks and tractors do the work that horses once did for people.

THE FIRST HORSE

The first horse, eohippus, was no bigger than a dog. Over millions of years, the horse has changed into the horse we know today.

A female horse is called a mare. A male horse is called a stallion. A young horse is called a foal.

WHERE HORSES LIVE

Horses live in all parts of the world except the colder regions near the North and South Poles.

KINDS OF HORSES

Draught horses are used to pull heavy loads.

Saddle horses are used for riding.

Ponies make good pets for children.

HOW A HORSE LIVES

• Foals can stand by themselves shortly after birth. They can run around after a few hours.
• A foal feeds on its mother's milk for six months.

• When a horse is one year old, it is half grown.
• Most horses reach full height and weight when they are about seven years old.
• Horses live for about 19 years.

HORSE RIDING

SEE ALSO • Hobby • Horse

Horse riding is a sport. People also ride horses as a hobby. Riders use their voices, hands and legs to tell a horse how to move.

A HORSE RIDER

A riders sits straight and relaxed in the saddle.

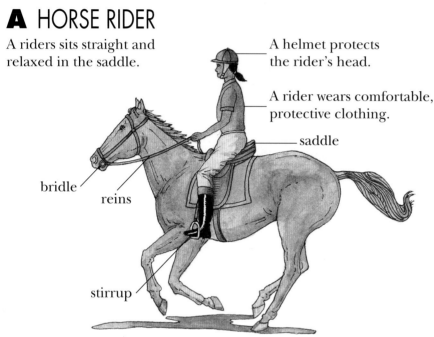

A helmet protects the rider's head.

A rider wears comfortable, protective clothing.

saddle

bridle

reins

stirrup

HOW A HORSE MOVES

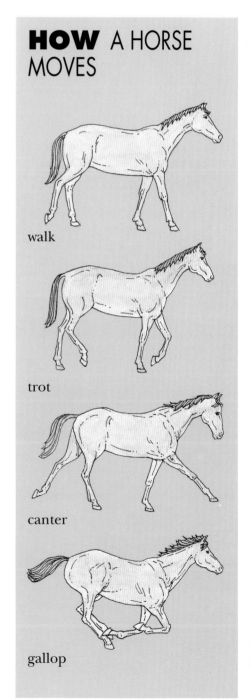

walk

trot

canter

gallop

HOW TO RIDE A HORSE

Mounting
A rider usually gets on to a horse from the left side.

Starting, turning and stopping
Riders can tell a horse to start, turn and stop by using their voice and gently pulling on the reins, and pushing their legs into the horse's side.

HORSE SHOWS ▶

Some people like to compete in horse shows. Jumping horses have very strong muscles to jump over hurdles.

. . . .

CARE OF A HORSE

A horse needs:
- shelter
- clean water every day
- fresh food every day
- grooming to keep healthy and neat
- regular exercise
- plenty of space for grazing and moving.

SOME GROOMING TOOLS

curry comb

hoof pick

dandy brush

sponge

hoof oil

body brush

INTERESTING FACT

Horseshoes protect a horse's hooves.

HORSE RACING ▼

Many people like to see horses compete in horse races.

HOSPITAL

SEE ALSO
• Ambulance • Doctor
• Drug • X-ray

A hospital is a place where sick and injured people are cared for. Many people work in a hospital to take care of the patients.

INSIDE A HOSPITAL

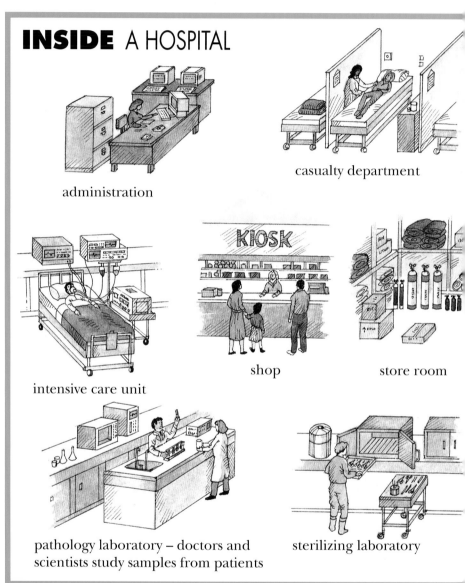

administration

casualty department

intensive care unit

shop

store room

pathology laboratory – doctors and scientists study samples from patients

sterilizing laboratory

CASUALTY DEPARTMENT

In the casualty department, medical care can be given very quickly to people who need it.

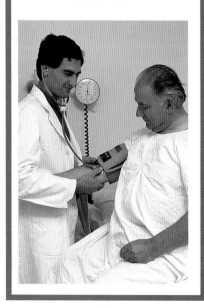

SPECIAL EQUIPMENT

In hospitals, different kinds of technical equipment such as scanning, X-ray and heart machines are used to help patients get better.

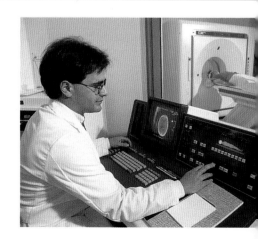

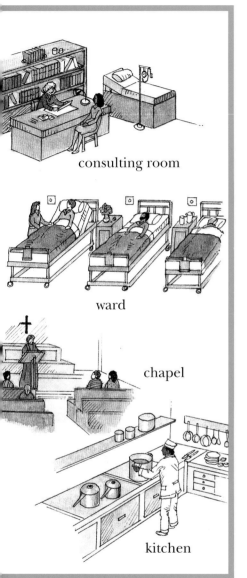

consulting room

ward

chapel

kitchen

OPERATING
THEATRE

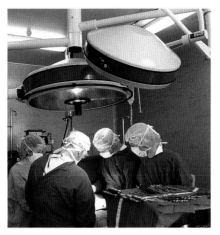

In the operating theatre, surgeons operate on sick people. Nurses help the surgeons. Everything in an operating theatre is sterilized so it is free from germs.

INTENSIVE
CARE UNIT

Intensive care units have special equipment for people who are very ill. An incubator is a special cot for a sick or tiny baby.

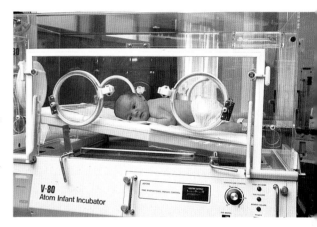

V-80
Atom Infant Incubator

WARDS

Several patients often share one ward. Sometimes, a patient has a separate room.

CHILDREN'S HOSPITAL

Children can play games and continue their school work while they are in hospital. Sometimes, their parents stay in hospital with them.

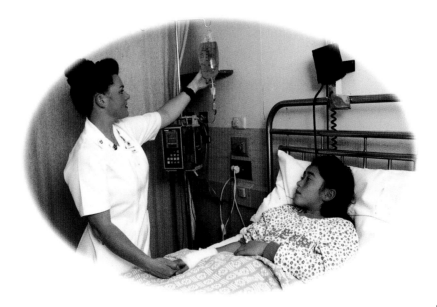

HOUSE

A house is a building that gives shelter and protection to people. It can keep out the rain and the cold or the heat.

SEE ALSO • Brick • Castle • Cave • Electricity • Garden

HISTORY

Long ago, people lived in caves. Caves sheltered people from the weather and protected them from wild animals.

HOUSES AROUND THE WORLD

HOUSE BOATS

In Hong Kong, some people live in boats called junks or sampans.

NOMADS' HOUSES

Nomads travel around with their animals to find new pastures. They live in portable homes such as tents.

HOW A WOODEN HOUSE IS BUILT

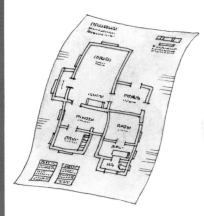

1. Builders use a plan to build a house.

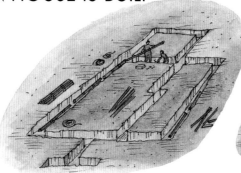

2. The foundations are laid. Pipes for water, sewerage, cables and electricity are put down in the foundations.

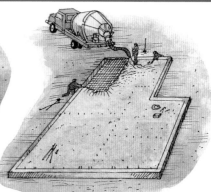

3. The floors are laid. Most floors are made of concrete or wood.

HIGH-RISE FLATS

Many families live in high-rise flats. High-rise flats are made of concrete. They are like lots of houses built on top of one another.

OLD MANSIONS

There are many beautiful old houses. Early settlers in America and Australia used wood they found in the forests to build their houses.

SNOW HOUSES

Inuits from the Arctic live in houses made of snow called igloos, when they are on winter expeditions.

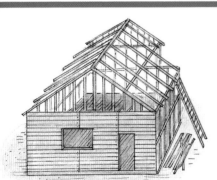

4. A frame for the house is built. Walls are attached to the frame. The walls are usually made of brick, concrete or wood and covered on the inside with plaster.

5. The roof is placed on top of the frame. Most roofs are sloped so rainwater runs into gutters. The roof is usually made of tin, tiles or slate.

6. Most houses have a number of rooms. Cupboards and doors are added to the inside of the house.

HOVERCRAFT

SEE ALSO
- Jet Engine • Ship
- Transport

A hovercraft is a vehicle that can travel on water and land. It rides on a cushion of air. A hovercraft can be driven by propellers or jet engines.

HOW A HOVERCRAFT WORKS

Powerful propellers drive a hovercraft forwards. Fans suck in air which is pumped under the hovercraft. Flaps or skirts hold the cushion of air under the hovercraft.

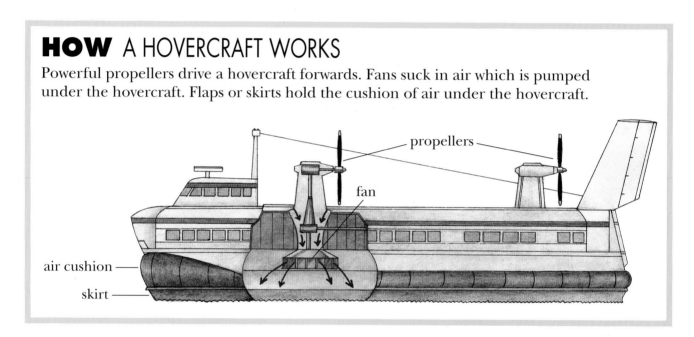

propellers

fan

air cushion

skirt

INTERESTING FACT

A hovercraft can travel at 120 kilometres an hour. It can travel faster than a ship.

A hovercraft can ▶ carry many passengers and cars smoothly and quickly across water.

SEE ALSO	• Brain • Digestion • Heart • Lungs • Skeleton • Skin

HUMAN BODY

The human body is made up of millions and millions of cells. Everyone's body looks different, but inside, our bodies are all the same. Each body has the same parts which work together.

ORGANS

Organs are a group of tissues that work together.
Your stomach, heart, lungs and skin are all organs. Organs work together in body systems.

BONES

Many organs like the heart and lungs are hidden behind bones. Bones protect these soft organs.

Tissues are made of groups of cells. Muscle tissues help you to lift things.

BODY SYSTEMS

These are some of the systems in your body.

RESPIRATORY SYSTEM

The nose, throat and lungs enable you to take in oxygen.

DIGESTIVE SYSTEM

The mouth, stomach and intestines break down the food you need for your body.

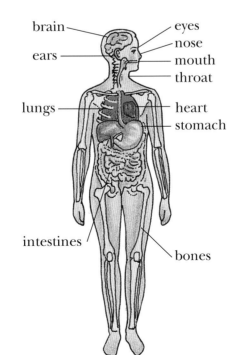

brain, eyes, nose, ears, mouth, throat, lungs, heart, stomach, intestines, bones

NERVOUS SYSTEM

The brain and nerves control your body.

CIRCULATORY SYSTEM

The heart, arteries and veins carry blood to all parts of your body.

55

ICEBERG

SEE ALSO
• Glacier

An iceberg is a huge, jagged block of ice that floats in the sea. It is part of a glacier that breaks off and drifts out to sea. Icebergs are found in the cold seas of the North and South Poles. Some weigh millions of tonnes.

MOVEMENT OF ICEBERGS

Icebergs are carried by sea currents and blown by winds. Some icebergs drift to warmer seas. Large icebergs can travel for thousands of kilometres and take several years to melt.

DANGER! ▲

Icebergs can be dangerous. In 1912, an ocean liner called the *Titanic* struck an iceberg and sank. About 1500 people were drowned.

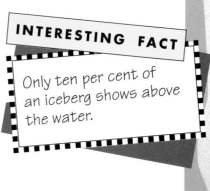

INTERESTING FACT

Only ten per cent of an iceberg shows above the water.

ICE SKATING

| SEE ALSO | • Hockey • Olympic Games • Skiing |

Ice skating is a sport. People wear special boots with blades on the bottom to skate on ice.

INDOOR ICE SKATING

In the past, ice skating was a winter sport. You could only skate in the winter months in the cold parts of the world.

Today, people can skate indoors at all times. At ice rinks, water is frozen to make ice for skaters.

KINDS OF ICE SKATING

Figure skating is when people perform spins, jumps and dance movements on ice.

Speed skating is racing on ice.

ICE SKATING AT ▶ THE OLYMPIC GAMES

Ice skaters in the Olympic Games perform spectacular jumps and spins.

INSECT

SEE ALSO
• Animal • Invertebrate
• Life Cycle • Nest

An insect is an animal. Insects are the largest group of animals on Earth. There are about one million different kinds of insects in the world.

PARTS OF AN INSECT

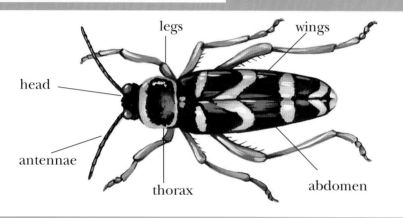

legs

wings

head

antennae

thorax

abdomen

Every insect has:
- three parts to its body – a head, a thorax and an abdomen
- two antennae
- an outer skeleton
- two to four wings
- three pairs of jointed legs.

LIFE CYCLES OF INSECTS

Insects can be divided into three groups with different life cycles.
All insects start life as eggs.

Silverfish

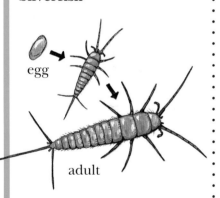

egg

adult

When these insects hatch, they look like the adults. As they grow bigger, they moult. They burst out of their outer skeleton and grow another one.

Grasshoppers

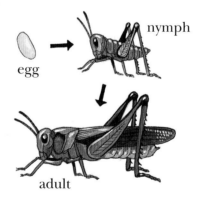

egg

nymph

adult

When these insects hatch, they look like adults. The young are called nymphs. As they grow, they moult. The last moult is the adult. They have wings.

Emperor gum moth

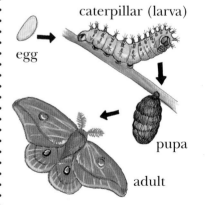

egg

caterpillar (larva)

pupa

adult

Butterflies and moths have four stages in their life cycle – egg, caterpillar or larva, pupa and moth or butterfly. Only the last adult stage has wings.

WINGS

Different insects have
different kinds
of wings.

• Butterflies and
moths have scaly wings.

• Beetles have hard,
protective wing cases.

• Many insects
such as bees,
flies, cicadas
and wasps
have wings with
fine membranes.

INSECTS ARE IMPORTANT

• Bees and many other flying
insects pollinate flowering
plants which produce fruit
and seeds.

• Honey bees make honey
which we can collect and eat.

• Scavenging insects such as
dung beetles eat decaying
matter. The waste matter
passed out by these insects
enriches the soil.

• Ladybirds are beetles which
feed on insect pests which
destroy plants.

• Silkworms make a silk
cocoon. Silk thread from
the cocoon is used to
make clothing.

HARMFUL INSECT PESTS

• Locusts can cause great
damage to crops.
• Mosquitoes and tsetse flies
can spread disease.
• Flies, lice, fleas and
cockroaches can damage
food or spread disease.

INTERESTING FACT

An insect's skeleton is
on the outside of its
body. It is called an
exoskeleton. It protects
the insect's soft body.

INVENTION

SEE ALSO
• Aeroplane • Machine
• Wheel

An invention is something new, created by a person. An invention can also be a new way of doing something. Some inventions are an improvement of something already invented.

Important inventions over the years have made great changes to our lives.

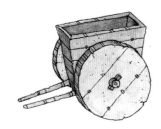

The wheel was invented about 3000 BC.

Gunpowder was invented by the Chinese in AD 1000.

The printing press was invented by Johannes Gutenberg in AD 1440.

The telephone was invented by Alexander Graham Bell in 1876.

The radio was invented by Guglielmo Marconi in 1895.

The first aeroplane to fly with an engine was invented by Wilbur and Orville Wright in 1903.

MODERN INVENTIONS

Inventions are often the work of a team of people. Today, teams of scientists, engineers and other inventors work together to find new inventions.

HELPFUL AND HARMFUL INVENTIONS

Many inventions have been helpful for people. Some inventions, such as the motor car, have been helpful but have made other problems such as pollution. Some inventions, such as war weapons, have been harmful to people.

INVERTEBRATE

| SEE ALSO | • Animal • Echinoderm
• Insect • Molluscs • Worm |

An invertebrate is an animal without a backbone.
Most animals on Earth are invertebrates.

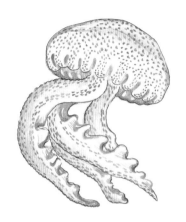

Some invertebrates such as
jellyfish have hollow bodies.

Protozoa are the
simplest group
of invertebrates.
They are a single
living cell. They are
so small, they can
only be seen using
a microscope. ▶

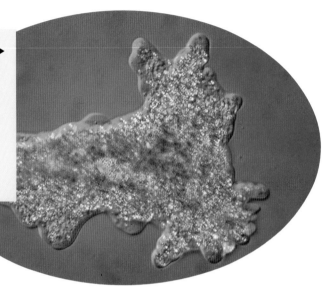

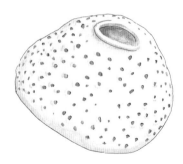

A sponge is a simple water
animal. It breathes and feeds
through holes on its body.

A snail has a soft, slimy body.
A hard shell on the outside
protects its body.

The biggest group of
invertebrates includes
spiders, insects
and crabs.

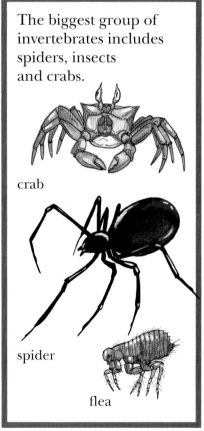

crab

spider

flea

Some invertebrates such as
the earthworm have a body
divided into segments.

Starfish are invertebrates
which move using small
tentacles called tube feet.

IRON AND STEEL

SEE ALSO • Bridge • Coal • Metal • Minerals • Mining • Rocks

Iron and steel are metals. Iron comes from the Earth's crust. Steel is made by mixing iron with carbon which comes from coal.

HISTORY ▶

During the Iron Age, thousands of years ago, people began to make knives, axes and swords out of iron.

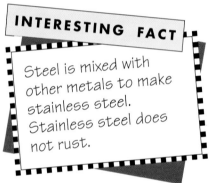

INTERESTING FACT

Steel is mixed with other metals to make stainless steel. Stainless steel does not rust.

◀ MINING IRON

Most iron is found in rocks in the ground. The rocks are dug out from the ground.

PRODUCTS MADE FROM IRON AND STEEL

Iron and steel are used to make machines that make nearly all the things we use.

machinery

tools

bridges

motor cars

bicycles

railway tracks

ships

HOW IRON AND STEEL ARE MADE

1. Iron is separated from rocks in a blast furnace. The iron melts in the blast furnace.

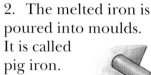

2. The melted iron is poured into moulds. It is called pig iron.

3. Steel is made by mixing iron and carbon which comes from coal.

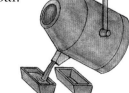

IRRIGATION

| SEE ALSO | • Dam • Farming |

Irrigation is a way of watering dry land so plants can grow. Irrigation makes it possible to grow crops and plants in dry places.

OLD METHODS OF IRRIGATION

Irrigation has been used for thousands of years to water plants in dry places. Today, people still use some of these methods such as digging wells or channels through fields to water crops.

MODERN ▼
IRRIGATION

Dams are often built across rivers to store water. Canals, ditches and pipes take the water to the fields.

ISLAND

SEE ALSO • Continent • Coral • Ocean • Volcano

An island is a piece of land surrounded by water.
Most islands are in the open ocean or sea.
Islands are also found in lakes and rivers.

CONTINENTAL ISLANDS

Continental islands were once part of a continent.

VOLCANIC ISLANDS

Volcanic islands are the tops of volcanoes that rise up from the seabed.

◄ CORAL CAYS

Coral cays are small islands. They are made from sand and coral which has built up over many years.

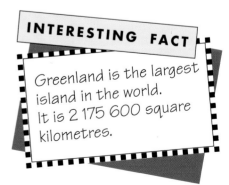

INTERESTING FACT

Greenland is the largest island in the world. It is 2 175 600 square kilometres.